First World War
and Army of Occupation
War Diary
France, Belgium and Germany

27 DIVISION
Divisional Troops
Royal Army Veterinary Corps
16 Mobile Veterinary Section
21 December 1914 - 19 July 1915

WO95/2259/5

The Naval & Military Press Ltd
www.nmarchive.com
Published in association with The National Archives

Published by

The Naval & Military Press Ltd

Unit 10 Ridgewood Industrial Park,

Uckfield, East Sussex,

TN22 5QE England

Tel: +44 (0) 1825 749494

www.naval-military-press.com

www.nmarchive.com

This diary has been reprinted in facsimile from the original. Any imperfections are inevitably reproduced and the quality may fall short of modern type and cartographic standards.

© **Crown Copyright**
Images reproduced by permission of The National Archives, London, England, 2015.

Contents

Document type	Place/Title	Date From	Date To
Heading	WO95/2259/5		
Heading	27th Division Divl Troops 16th Mobile Vety Section Dec 1914-Jly 1915		
Heading	27th Division 16th Mobile Vety, Section Vol I Dec 1914-Feb 1915		
War Diary		21/12/1914	23/12/1914
War Diary	Arques	24/12/1914	08/01/1915
War Diary	Boeschepe	08/01/1915	28/02/1915
Heading	27th Division 16th Mobile Vetenary Section Vol II 1-31.3.15		
War Diary	Boeschepe	01/03/1915	31/03/1915
War Diary		01/04/1915	31/05/1915
Heading	27th Division 16th Mobile Vety Section Vol III June 1-4-30.6.15		
War Diary		01/06/1915	30/06/1915
Heading	27th Division 16th Mobile Vety Section Vol IV From 1st To 31st July 1915		
War Diary		20/07/1915	31/07/1915
War Diary		01/07/1915	19/07/1915

W095/2259/5

27TH DIVISION
DIVL TROOPS

16TH MOBILE VETY SECTION
DEC 1914-JLY 1915

121/4716

27th Division

16th Kiotid Telg: Section

Vol I

Dec 1914 — Feb 1915

Page No 1

WAR DIARY
or
INTELLIGENCE SUMMARY.
(Erase heading not required.)

Army Form C. 2118.

Hour, Date, Place	Summary of Events and Information	Remarks and references to Appendices
10.30 a.m. December 21st 1914	Left Winchester en route for Southampton.	
5 p.m. " " "	Arrived at Southampton.	
8 p.m. " " "	Embarked on Trafford Hall.	
10 p.m. " " "	Left Southampton.	
6 a.m. December 22nd 1914	Arrived off Havre.	
10 a.m. " " "	Disembarked. Billeted in Hangar U. Horsefighted	
	Got close to the Hangar. Street Leopold joined	
1. c.p.m. December 25th 1914	Entrained.	
2. 15 am December 27th 1914	Arrived at Arques & detrained	
3. 9 a.m December 28th 1914	Billeted in Schoolroom. Horse picketed in the yard	
December 28th 1914	Put down lines for collecting sick & injured horses.	
" 27th	Collected 3 horses.	
" 28th	Collected 7 horses.	
" 29th	Collected 31 horses. Refected by tow.	
" 30th	3 horses died.	
" 31st	Collected 2 horses. Refected tow.	
January 1st 1915	Collected 5 horses.	
" 2nd "	Collected 12 horses.	15 horses to N.E. Que Ret.
January 3rd "	Collected 14 horses. One horse cuice & skinned before destroyed.	6.E. 16 Quebec

Page No 2

WAR DIARY
or
INTELLIGENCE SUMMARY.
(Erase heading not required.)

Army Form C. 2118.

Hour, Date, Place	Summary of Events and Information	Remarks and references to Appendices
January 4th 1915	Admitted 24 horses. One horse died, two destroyed, one left with Civil Authorities & 64 evacuated.	
January 5th 1915	Rejected by A.D.V.S.	
" 6th 1915	Collected 4 horses. Seven cured & returned. One died.	
P.Sam January 7th 1915	Collected 1 horse. One died. One left with Civil Authorities.	
Cagette 12 gm " " "	Left Agnes	
P.40 am " 8th "	Arrived at Croisette. Billetted for the night in farm	
Directly " "	Reached from Croisette passing through Bailleuxbapaume	L.J. Junket from Lychett
11.30 P.m. " "	Avesne lez Bailleul ag.am Coupel & Bretteren	L.E. 16 Not set
	Arrived at Beauchife. 20 tired horses. Billetted in	
	Yebleyson	
January 9th 1915	Lines down prepared to collect horses. No beshorse arr.	
January 10th 1915	Moved to first billet in a farm. Rat also lives & electricity.	
	Collected 3 horses. No petrol noise of traverse laving	
January 11th 1915	Red. R.Q. Signal & infantry	
	Collected 2 horses	
January 12th 1915	Collected 5 horses. Cured & returned two horses	
	Rejected by A.D.V.S.	
January 13th 1915	Collected 1 horse. Received 70-remounts	
January 14th 1915	Collected 5 horses. Cured & returned one horse. Issued 70-remounts	
	Rejected horses of Divisional Cavalry & H.Q Signal Company, to	
January 16th 1915	Collected 2 horses. Cured & returned one horse. Two horses died.	

WAR DIARY or INTELLIGENCE SUMMARY.

Army Form C. 2118.

(Erase heading not required.)

Hour, Date, Place	Summary of Events and Information	Remarks and references to Appendices
January 16th 1916	Collected 3 horses. Cured & Returned 5 horses. One died. Inspected by ADVS. Looked for new billets at Hebuterne.	Lost my last shaving kit. Latrines are C.de.L. Here this is a new fad and the Officers in a day had created a big Latrines and Cookhouse not in attic.
January 17th 1916	Not found nothing available.	
January 18th 1915	Collected 12 horses. Inspected horses of Divisional Cavalry and H.Q. Signal Company.	
January 19th 1916	Collected 3 horses.	
January 20th 1916	Collected 5 horses. One horse died. Received 32 remounts.	
January 21st 1916	Issued 32 remounts.	
January 22nd 1916	Collected 8 horses. One horse died. Evacuated 16 horses.	
January 23rd 1916	Inspected by ADVS.	
January 24th 1916	Collected 10 horses. Destroyed one horse. Inspected horses of Divisional Cavalry & H.Q. Signal Company.	
January 25th 1916	Collected 11 horses. One died. One destroyed.	
January 26th 1916	Collected 7 horses. Cured & Returned 2. Died 1. Evacuated 26.	
January 27th 1916	Collected 5 horses. Inspected horses of Divisional Cavalry & H.Q. Signal Coy.	
January 28th 1916	Collected 5 horses. Inspected by ADVS.	
January 29th 1916	Collected 14 horses. Cured & Returned two horses.	
January 30th 1916	Collected 13 horses. Evacuated 20 horses.	
January 31st 1916	Collected 14 horses. Cured & Returned one. Destroyed one. Evacuated 27. Received 21 remounts.	
	Inspected horses of Divisional Cavalry, HQ Signal Company. Collected 2 horses. Issued 31 remounts. Inspected by ADVS.	

Army Form C. 2118.

WAR DIARY
or
INTELLIGENCE SUMMARY.
(Erase heading not required.)

Instructions regarding War Diaries and Intelligence Summaries are contained in F.S. Regs., Part II. and the Staff Manual respectively. Title pages will be prepared in manuscript.

Hour, Date, Place	Summary of Events and Information	Remarks and references to Appendices
February 1st 1915	Collected 6 horses.	
February 2nd 1915	Collected 8 horses.	
February 3rd 1915	Collected 9 horses. Cured & relieved one. Evacuated 1h.	
February 4th 1915	Collected 5 horses. Cured ~~destroyed~~ one. Destroyed one.	
February 5th 1915	Collected 5 horses. Destroyed one. Inspected horses of Divisional Cavalry. 7 H.Q. Signal Company.	
February 6th 1915	Collected 8 horses. Evacuated 16. Inspected by ADVS.	
February 7th 1915	Collected 12 horses. Cured & relieved one.	
February 8th 1915	Collected 6 horses. Inspected Divisional Cavalry.	
February 9th 1915	Collected 10 horses. Destroyed one.	
February 10th 1915	Collected 4 horses. Cured one.	
February 11th 1915	Collected 7 horses. Sick one.	
February 12th 1915	Collected 3 horses. Destroyed 2. Evacuated 15. Inspected by ADVS.	D.D. Inspector
February 13th 1915	Collected 7 horses. Inspected horses of Divisional Cavalry.	
February 14th 1915	Inspected by DDVS.	
February 15th 1915	Collected 10 horses. Destroyed one. Evacuated 16.	
February 16th 1915	Collected 6 horses. Evacuated one.	
February 17th 1915	Collected 10 horses. Inspected horses of Divisional Cavalry;	
February 18th 1915	Collected 9 horses. Issued to new billet.	
February 19th 1915	Collected 7 horses. Destroyed two.	
February 20th 1915	Collected 18 horses. Evacuated 9h. Inspected Divisional Cavalry. Received signed documents.	
February 21st 1915	Collected 13 horses. Destroyed two. Sergt Buchanan left for Veterinary Hospital.	
February 22nd 1915	Collected 6 horses. Inspected by ADVS.	

Army Form C. 2118.

Page No 5

WAR DIARY
or
INTELLIGENCE SUMMARY.
(Erase heading not required.)

Instructions regarding War Diaries and Intelligence Summaries are contained in F. S. Regs., Part II and the Staff Manual respectively. Title pages will be prepared in manuscript.

One 6/6

Hour, Date, Place	Summary of Events and Information	Remarks and references to Appendices
February 23rd 1916	Collected 10 horses. Tried 2, destroyed one. Proved to be —	
February 24th 1916	Pilot on Mr. Beradage.	
	Collected 2 horses. Inspected by ADVR.	
February 25th 1916	Collected 7 horses. Evacuated 82.	
February 26th 1916	Collected 27 horses. Inspected Divisional Cavalry.	
February 27th 1916	Collected 6 horses. Inspected Transport Animals of 9th Argyll & Sutherland 4/1st Cambridge. Left Newark. Horse of 1st Cambridge with Hanover at Sedbergham & York Ave. Government Lorr from Mr. Hanover & landed men to 1st Cambridge. Rupees Cambely. Handed 8 sick horses of 1/5 Cambridge to 16 Mobile Veterinary Section. Evacuated A.S. Inspected by ADVR.	Bad weather throughout the month. Horses in not as January here here are fine.
February 28th 1916	Collected 2 horses. Tried one.	

J Chamberlain
O.C. 16 Mobile Section

131/4893.

27th Division

16th Mobile Veterinary Section

Vol II 1 – 31.3.15

WAR DIARY or INTELLIGENCE SUMMARY.

Army Form C. 2118.

(Erase heading not required.)

Page No. 1

Hour, Date, Place	Summary of Events and Information	Remarks and references to Appendices
Boulsie Ypres November 1915	Inspected by ADVS. Collected 18 horses. Cured & returned 1, destroyed 1.	
" 2nd "	Collected 13 horses. Fired 1.	
" 3rd "	Collected 3 horses. Fired 2. 1 Sergeant S.Sergeant & Sergeant delegate to rejoin to	
" 4th "	Moved to No.10 Base Hospital	
" 5th "	Collected 12 horses. 1 Sergeant & Sergeant delegate to 5th Veterinary Hospital. Inspected Transport animals of 1st Cambridge.	
" 6th "	Collected 9 horses. Destroyed 2. Inspected by ADVS.	
" 7th "	Inspected Divisional Cavalry horses.	
" 8th "	Collected 1 horse.	
" 9th "	Collected 5 horses. Cured & returned 2. Destroyed 2.	
" 10th "	Inspected by DDVS. Collected 7 horses. Fired 1.	
" 11th "	Inspected Divisional Cavalry. Collected 15 horses. Destroyed 3.	
" 12th "	Collected 1 horse. Cured 3. Evacuated 3.	
" 13th "	Collected 7 horses. Destroyed 1. Inspected Divisional Cavalry horses.	
" 14th "	Inspected by ADVS. Collected 15 horses. Received 40 remounts.	
" 15th "	Collected 9 horses. Fired 1. Issued remounts.	
" 16th "	Collected 9 horses. Inspected Divisional Cavalry. Received remounts.	
" 17th "	Evacuated 1 remount. Collected 18 horses. Evacuated 3.	
" 18th "	Fired 1. Collected 8 horses. Destroyed 3. Received wounded 12 remounts.	
" 19th "	Inspected by ADVS. Collected 12 horses. Received 4 remounts.	
" 20th "	Collected 18 horses. Cured & returned 1. Destroyed 1. Issued 4 remounts.	
	Received 14 remounts. Issued 12 remounts. Inspected by DVS	

Page N° 2

WAR DIARY
or
INTELLIGENCE SUMMARY.
(Erase heading not required.)

Army Form C. 2118.

Hour, Date, Place	Summary of Events and Information	Remarks and references to Appendices
Boeschepe March 19th 1916	Collected 3 horses. Destroyed 1. Evacuated 6.6. Inspected Divisional Cavalry horses.	
" 20th "	Inspected R.A.D.W.	
" 21st "	Collected 10 horses. Inspected Divisional Cavalry horses.	
" 22nd "	Collected 8 horses. Destroyed 1.	
" 23rd "	Collected 7 horses. Cast & destroyed 2. Destroyed 1.	
" 24th "	Inspected Divisional Cavalry. Cpl. Baker & Lgan. left for No 9 Base Hospital.	
" 25th "	Collected 14 horses. Cast & rejected 2. Destroyed 1. Evacuated 67.	
" " "	Pte Grier & Mudie sent to Church & about Frostbite.	
" 26th "	Collected 4 horses. Remounted Pte Jones fr ADW at 11am 26th inst.	
" " "	Collected 4 horses. Pte Joyce two horses left for A.D.W. Evacuated #22 day.	
" " "	No 2 Field Ambulance.	
" 27th "	Collected 6 horses. Inspected Divisional Cavalry horses.	Considerable improvement in the weather, chief consequent rise in near for better condition of men & ADW.
" 28th "	Collected 3 horses. Inspected by ADW. Pte. Ratcliff & Pte Grinners	
" " "	Inoculation.	
" 29th "	Collected 8 horses.	
" 30th "	Collected 9 horses. Destroyed 2. Evacuated #20. Inspected by ADW.	J.J. [signature]
" 31st "	Inspected Divisional Cavalry. Collected 1 horse.	[signature]

Army Form C. 2118.

WAR DIARY
or
INTELLIGENCE SUMMARY.
(Erase heading not required.)

16. M.V.S.

Hour, Date, Place	Summary of Events and Information	Remarks and references to Appendices
April 1st 1916	Admitted 16 sick horses. Evacuated 22.	
2nd "	Admitted 9 sick horses. Collected one horse left in October for	
3rd "	Farm at Steenwerck.	
4th "	Admitted 2 sick horses.	
5th "	Moved section to new billet between Dopringhe & Vlamertinghe.	
6th "	Left 5 sick horses which were unable to move with No 11 M.V.S.	
7th "	Wrote to Railhead to arrange with RTO about trucks for	
8th "	sick horses.	
9th "	Routine. Inspected Divisional Cavalry.	
10th "	Admitted 1 sick horse. Inspected by ADVS. One horse cured & returned.	
11th "	Routine.	
12th "	Admitted 9 sick horses.	
13th "	Admitted 2 sick horses. Evacuated 18. Attended conference	
	5 VOs at Div office 4 P.M. Gas.	
14th "	Inspected by DVS. Destroyed one horse of Divisional Cavalry	
	which had a fracture from a kick. SP Pte	J Smith 2 MC
15th "	Admitted 21 sick horses. #t. L.E. AO 2070, Whitehall & JE	J Smith x Peter
	No 2096 Pte Murray joined the section.	
16th "	Evacuated 2 sick horses. Inspected Divisional Cavalry horses.	
17th "	Admitted 3 sick horses.	
18th "	Admitted 1 sick horse.	
19th "	Evacuated 20 horses. One horse cured & returned.	
20th "	Collected 2 sick horses. One long cured & returned.	C 16 Metcalfe
	Collected 2 horse from Doctor. ADVS killed by shell fire.	

Army Form C. 2118.

WAR DIARY
or
INTELLIGENCE SUMMARY.
(Erase heading not required.)

Instructions regarding War Diaries and Intelligence Summaries are contained in F.S. Regs. Part II. and the Staff Manual respectively. Title pages will be prepared in manuscript.

Hour, Date, Place	Summary of Events and Information	Remarks and references to Appendices
April 21st 1915	Admitted 12 sick & one. Collected one from Farm at Poperinghe. Evacuated 11 sick & one. Cared & removed 1. Station standing to all night.	
22nd		
23rd	Admitted 1 sick & one. Inspected trains of Divisional Cavalry.	
24th	Admitted 8 sick & one. Cured & removed 1.	
25th	Admitted 18 sick & one. Destroyed 2.	
26th	Admitted 17 sick & one. Evacuated 2. D.A.D.V.S. who helped at off of the case. & lined with the Section. Cured & removed one horse.	
27th	Admitted 11 sick & one. Evacuated 4 sick horses. Visit from D.D.V.S. 2nd Army. Inspected Divisional Train.	
28th	Admitted 1 sick & one. Evacuated 23. Visit D.D.V.S. 2nd Army.	
29th	Admitted 8 sick & one. Destroyed 1. Visit D.D.V.S. 2nd Army. Inspected Divisional Train & Divisional Cavalry.	
30th	Admitted 14 sick & one. Evacuated 31. Cured & removed 1.	

J.G. .... to A.V.C.
L.C.16 Mobile Vety Section

Army Form C. 2118.

WAR DIARY
or
INTELLIGENCE SUMMARY.
(Erase heading not required.)

3 16 MVS

Instructions regarding War Diaries and Intelligence Summaries are contained in F.S. Regs., Part II and the Staff Manual respectively. Title pages will be prepared in manuscript.

Hour, Date, Place	Summary of Events and Information	Remarks and references to Appendices
May 1st 1916	Admitted 36 sick horses. Destroyed 1. Inspected Divisional train.	
2nd	Admitted 2 sick horses. Evacuated 32. Inspected Divisional Cavalry.	
3rd	Admitted 10 sick horses. Evacuated 40. Destroyed 1.	
4th	Collected 4 sick horses. Evacuated 32. Destroyed 2. Died 1.	
5th	Cured & reissued 1.	
6th	Admitted 12 sick horses. Evacuated 82. Destroyed 2. Inspected Divisional Train	
7th	Collected 31 sick horses. Destroyed 1. Cured & reissued 1. Inspected Divisional Cavalry.	
8th	Collected 2 horses. Evacuated 32.	
	Admitted 9 sick horses. Destroyed 2. Cured & reissued 1.	
	Recommended No 968 Cpl Machin H.T. to be Sergeant. No 391 LCpl Stanley to be Corporal & Pte No 1205 Pte Boiven N.C.T. to be Corporal & Pte No 906 Pte Wyatt A to be Corporal.	
9th	Admitted 14 sick horses. Inspected Divisional Train.	
10th	Admitted 8 sick horses & evacuated 26. Cured & reissued 2.	
11th	Admitted 9 sick horses. Inspected Divisional Cavalry.	
12th	Admitted 20 sick horses. Destroyed 1. Died 1. No 391 LCpl Stanley left action for No 8 Convalescent Horse Depot.	
13th	Admitted 2 sick horses. Evacuated 24. Destroyed 1.	
14th	Admitted Patch horse. Died 1. Inspected train & Cavalry horses. New 1 heavy draught horse from A.D. Ly Train.	
16th	Admitted 9 & destroyed 1. Collected 2 Convalescent horses from Govt Champbetin Broeschepe.	

(73989) W4141—463. 400,000. 9/14. H.&J.Ltd. Forms/C. 2118/10.

Army Form C. 2118.

WAR DIARY
or
INTELLIGENCE SUMMARY.
(Erase heading not required.)

Instructions regarding War Diaries and Intelligence Summaries are contained in F.S. Regs., Part II and the Staff Manual respectively. Title pages will be prepared in manuscript.

Hour, Date, Place	Summary of Events and Information	Remarks and references to Appendices
May 16th 1916	Admitted 6 sick horses. Evacuated 1 P. S.E. No. 1171. S.S. Philippson	
17th	Joined the Section.	
18th	Admitted 6 sick horses. Destroyed 1. Inspected Divisional Train.	
	Admitted 6 sick horses. Destroyed 1. No. 256 Off. Machine HH	
19th	Promoted Sergeant.	
20th	Admitted 4 sick horses. Inspected Divisional Cavalry.	
21st	Admitted 2 sick horses. Evacuated 19.	
22nd	Admitted 7 sick horses.	
	Admitted 8 sick horses. Inspected Train & Corn Column.	
	New Interpreter arrived.	
23rd	Admitted 4 sick horses. Cured & reissued 1. New 2 recruits.	
	New Ammunition Column. Cast from DD rs 2nd Army.	
24th	Admitted 5 sick horses. Destroyed 1. Shot 1.	
25th	Admitted 6 sick horses. Evacuated 19. Destroyed 1. Inspected	
	Divisional Cavalry	
26th	Admitted 13 sick horses. Inspected train horses.	
27th	Admitted 9 sick horses. Cured & reissued 1. Inspected	
	24 ADvs.	
28th	Admitted 2 sick horses. Evacuated 26.	
29th	Admitted 10 sick horses. Inspected Train & Cavalry horses.	Sgt Oncher ? W.C.
30th	Evacuated 0 sick horses.	T.C./6 Machine
31st	Admitted 4 sick horses. Cured & reissued 1. Handed over 2.	
	Set on Mund Marched via Bouzeleg, Bethune, Hingin	
	Cuffies, Bazelyl, & Stannick to Cand Wilsat Ervire Lakre,	
	No. No. 902, S.E. Reaves, No. No. 2020. Pte Fairley 25? No. A 860 Pts Puthills	
	Leton. Joined the Section for duty.	

(73989) W4141—463. 400,000. 9/14. H.&J.Ltd. Forms/C. 2118/10.

121/6390

27th Division

18th Infantry Brigade Section
Vol III
from 4-30-6-15
June

WAR DIARY or INTELLIGENCE SUMMARY.

Army Form C. 2118.

16th M.V.S.

Hour, Date, Place	Summary of Events and Information	Remarks and references to Appendices
June 1st 1915	Admitted 4 sick horses. Inspected Divisional Cavalry & Train horses. No. 368 Sergeant Machin H.H. left station to join Indian Veterinary Hospital Rouen.	
June 2nd 1915	Admitted 10 sick horses.	
3rd	Admitted 6 sick horses. Evacuated 16. Destroyed 1. Inspected Divisional Train & Cavalry horses. Recommended No. 36 Sergeant Moretin H.H. to be Staff Sergeant, S.E. No. 1232 Acting Corporal Barnes to be Corporal, No. 4905 Pte Boyliff G.H.F.G. (attached 16 MVS) to be Corporal. S.P.E. 1120 Seely J.S. to be Lance Corporal.	
4th	Admitted 6 sick horses. Collected one loose farm horse at Bracegate Stewart.	
5th	Admitted 6 sick horses. Destroyed 1.	
6th	Admitted 27 sick horses. Inspected Divisional Train and Cavalry horses.	
7th	Admitted 16 sick horses. Evacuated 38.	
8th	Admitted 1 sick horse. Inspected Train & Cavalry horses.	
9th	Admitted 18 sick horses. Destroyed 2. Fired 1.	
10th	Admitted 6 sick horses. Evacuated 26. Destroyed 1,	
11th	Admitted 8 sick horses. Inspected Train & Cavalry horses.	
12th	Admitted 21 sick horses.	
13th	Admitted 8 sick horses. Evacuated 38.	
14th	Admitted 4 sick horses.	
16th	Admitted 12 sick horses.	
16th	Inspected sick horses. Inspected by DDVS 2nd Army.	
17th	Inspected Train & Cavalry horses.	

Army Form C. 2118.

WAR DIARY
or
INTELLIGENCE SUMMARY.
(Erase heading not required.)

6

Hour, Date, Place	Summary of Events and Information	Remarks and references to Appendices
June 18th 1916	Admitted 3 sick horses. Evacuated 22. War Staff Capt 82rd Inf Bde re use of rifle range for instruction of NCOs & men of the Bde.	
19th		
20th	Admitted 6 sick horses. Inspected Train & Cavalry horses.	
21st	Admitted 5 sick horses. Cured & reissued 4.	
22nd	Admitted Bath horses. Cured & reissued 1. Admitted 3 sick horses. Visit to mem N Coy Queen of Cavalry to rifle range for practice. Inspected train & Cavalry horses.	
23rd	Admitted 6 sick horses. Inspected train horses.	
24th	Admitted 4 sick horses. Evacuated 18.	
25th	Routine. Inspected train & Cavalry horses.	
26th	Admitted 6 sick horses. Collected ne mess of two men horses at Ammunitions. Inspected Cavalry horses.	
27th	Admitted 4 sick horses. Inspected train & Cavalry horses. Routine. Visit from DDVS 2nd Army.	J G Mikhail Lt vet Sgn
28th	Admitted 3 sick horses. Inspected train & Cavalry horses.	C 16 M H Vet for
29th	Admitted 10 sick horses. Evacuated 26.	
30th	Took 12 NCos & men of section to rifle range for practice.	

121/6437

27th Division

16th hostile Batty: Sector

Vol IV

From 1st to 31st July 1915.

Army Form C. 2118.

WAR DIARY
or
INTELLIGENCE SUMMARY. 2
(Erase heading not required.)

July 1915

Hour, Date, Place	Summary of Events and Information	Remarks and references to Appendices
July 20th 1915	Admitted 1 sick horse. Inspected Divisional Train & Cavalry horses.	
" 21st 1915	Admitted 7 sick horses. S.S. No. 4360 S.S. Smettilley J.A. left the doctor with order to report to O.C Veterinary Section N.Zeal Cavalry Brigade.	
" 22nd "	Admitted 4 sick horses. Inspected Divisional Cavalry horses.	
" 23rd "	Admitted 5 sick horses. Inspected Divisional Train horses.	
" 24th "	Inspected Divisional Train & Cavalry horses.	
" 25th "	Routine.	
" 26th "	Admitted 1 sick horse. Evacuated 16 S.S. No. 3784 Pte Grant J.H.	
" 27th "	Joined doctor from No. 6 Veterinary Hospital.	
" 28th "	Admitted 4 sick horses. Inspected Divisional Cavalry.	
" 29th "	Admitted 1 sick horse.	
" 30th "	Admitted 6 sick horses. Inspected Divisional Cavalry.	
" 31st "	Evacuated & Reigned to horses. Routine. Inspected Divisional Cavalry horses. Admitted 16 sick horses.	

Army Form C. 2118.

WAR DIARY July 1915
or
INTELLIGENCE SUMMARY. 1
(Erase heading not required.)

Instructions regarding War Diaries and Intelligence Summaries are contained in F.S. Regs., Part II and the Staff Manual respectively. Title pages will be prepared in manuscript.

Hour, Date, Place	Summary of Events and Information	Remarks and references to Appendices
July 1st 1915	Admitted 6 sick horses. Inspected Divisional Train horses.	
" 2nd "	Admitted 6 sick horses. Inspected Divisional Cavalry horses.	
" 3rd "	Admitted 5 sick horses. Evacuated 17.	
" 4th "	Admitted 6 sick horses. Inspected Divisional Ammunition Column horses, also Divisional Train horses.	
" 5th "	Admitted 5 sick horses. Fired 1. Inspected by A.D.V.S. Inspected Divisional Cavalry horses.	
" 6th "	Admitted 1 sick horse. Died 1.	
" 7th "	Admitted 6 sick horses.	
" 8th "	Admitted 2 sick horses. Inspected Divisional Train horses.	
" 9th "	Admitted 1 sick horse. Evacuated 19.	
" 10th "	Admitted 1 sick horse. Inspected Divisional Cavalry horses. Cast 2.	
" 11th "	Admitted 2 sick horses. Wounded 2.	
" 12th "	Admitted 9 sick horses.	
" 13th "	Admitted 16 sick horses. Destroyed 1. Inspected Divisional Train horses.	S.S. 2090 Pte Brinn, G. L. Hospital
" 14th "	Admitted 5 sick horses. Evacuated 20.	
" 15th "	Admitted 5 sick horses. Inspected Divisional Cavalry.	
" 16th "	Routine. Inspected Divisional Cavalry horses.	
" 17th "	Admitted 6 sick horses.	
" 18th "	Admitted 4 sick horses. Inspected Divisional Train & Cavalry horses.	
" 19th "	Admitted 3 sick horses. Inspected Divisional Train horses.	
" 20th "	Admitted 5 sick horses. Evacuated 22. No 4336 Pte R.E. Grinn P. 6th Dragoon Guards left Leton with orders to report to O.C. Cavalry Reinforcements Rouen.	

www.ingramcontent.com/pod-product-compliance
Lightning Source LLC
Chambersburg PA
CBHW081508160426
43193CB00014B/2622